BOOM

A True Story of Perseverance, Mental Toughness,
and Overcoming Adversity

RANDY "BOOM BOOM" BLAKE

Five-Time World Champion Kickboxer

26 25 24 23 22   10 9 8 7 6 5 4 3 2 1

BOOM–– A True Story Of Perseverance, Mental Toughness, And Overcoming Adversity From The 5-Time World Champion Kickboxer.
©2022 RANDY BLAKE

All Rights Reserved. Except as permitted under the U.S. Copyright Act of 1976, no part of this publication may be reproduced, distributed, or transmitted in any form by any means, or stored in a database or retrieval system, without the prior written permission of the author and/or publisher.

Published by:
Emerge Publishing, LLC
9521 B Riverside parkway, Suite 243
Tulsa, OK 74137
Phone: 888.407.4447
www.emerge.pub

Library of Congress Cataloging-in-Publication Data:
ISBN: 978-1954966-18-5 Perfect Bound
E-book available exclusively on Kindle

BISAC:
SPO027010   SPORTS & RECREATION / Martial Arts / Karate
SPO027000   SPORTS & RECREATION / Martial Arts / General SPO066000
SPORTS & RECREATION / Cultural & Social Aspects

Photo Credits:
Front Cover Image: Tia Dawn Photography
Back Cover Image: Jennifer Dubler Photography

Printed in the United States

CONTENTS

INTRODUCTION

Boom! As my kick landed on his ribs, I felt a surge inside of me. Every athlete that has trained for "the moment" and has successfully made it to the pinnacle of their personal quest, where they can then set themselves apart from all the others, feels something similar. For some it's the Olympics, for others it's the Super Bowl. For me, it was fighting Mike Sheppard for the ISKA International Sport Karate Association World Heavyweight Championship in 2012 in Tulsa, Oklahoma.

Whack! My punch landed and then the final moment of the match was a flying knee. That brought gushes of blood from Mike's face, and the fight was called. I was the ISKA World Champion!

Many times, the story of how someone got their start in the fighting world is linked to a point where the guy was in trouble of some sort. A tough family life, fighting at school, or maybe even on his way to prison.

If I walked into your coffee shop right now, or your home, or wherever you find yourself reading the pages of this book, you probably wouldn't pay much attention. If you happened to look up, and we made eye contact, I would smile at you and you'd likely smile back.

I've met countless people who know I'm a fighter, and they've all said the same thing: "Randy, you definitely don't look or act like I was thinking you would. You are so laid back and chill. You have a great smile, and you're so easy to carry on a conversation with."

I never saw myself as a champion. Don't get me wrong, I'm not saying I had some horrible upbringing that I had to overcome or something like that. In fact, I grew up with parents who loved me and loved each other, and life was fairly average. So, when one of my instructors said, "Randy, you ought to try a fight class. You need to see what it feels like to hit somebody!" I wasn't out for blood or even thinking about kickboxing as a career.

As I share my story of world titles and the kickboxing life, I want to lead you on a journey of five principles that made me the man I am today. They are taken from the practice of martial arts. They are **Courage, Discipline, Perseverance, Respect and Integrity.**

Many training studios have their own version of these, but I wanted to include the ones that have been with me throughout my career and my life.

As you read the stories of how the principles apply to various parts of my life, hopefully you can find yourself somewhere in these pages. Let this idea sink into your soul: if you feel like you're lacking somewhere, you can pick any of these principles up right now and make them a part of your life. It's as simple as making a decision to change. Keep in mind a few tenets we learn in training for martial arts: patience and consistency.

Wherever you find yourself in life right now, whether it be in a beautiful home surrounded by family and kids or a broken home, feeling broken, as you flip through the pages of my story, I hope you'll be encouraged when you're finished. I am here to encourage you that anything is possible!

ROUND ONE

COURAGE

"He who is not courageous enough to take risks
will accomplish nothing in life."
-Muhammad Ali

When I was a kid growing up in Cleveland, Ohio, I didn't have the sense of courage and pride that I do today. I grew up in an interesting household. I had both parents at home. My mom was the facilitator and farmer in my life. She sowed seeds that would eventually grow for me to harvest later in life. My father had a successful career, as well as being a welder and exterminator. Living in Ohio, for whatever reason, I just never seemed to fit in. I always felt like I was different. Not that it was bad to be different, it was just hard for me to fit in.

Average is how I would describe myself when I was a kid. I wasn't the smallest, but I wasn't the biggest. I was quiet and unassuming. I hadn't found my voice in those early years of my life. I know that's not something unusual because most kids are just trying to find their way in their early years. But for me, I would just go with the flow and try not to make any waves or disturb things too much. Going with the flow is fine if you're referring to a river, but not always with life.

Going with the flow is fine if you're referring to a river, but not always with life. I have a vivid memory illustrating this idea from when I was in elementary school. Every single day, a boy would find me, put me in a headlock and punch me in the gut. I always heard some weird noise he'd make with his mouth… and then he would walk away. Every. Single. Day. It never occurred to me to stop him. In my mind, I was thinking the best way to deal with him was to let him get it over with and go about my day. I did everything possible to avoid drawing attention to myself. I know it may sound crazy now, but at the time it worked.

I had no idea what was happening during those

momentary headlocks. One day, my aunt picked me up from school, and as I climbed into her car she remarked, "What in the world is in your hair?" I was trying to avoid the conversation, but I replied, "What are you talking about?" She told me to bend my head down. When I did, she gasped and said it was full of spit, boogers, loogies and spit wads. She angrily asked, "Who did that?!"

Little did I know, that kid's 15-second headlock was filling my hair with all that junk! Here's the kicker...I *didn't* shift in strategy at that point to stand up for myself and say, "I'm not gonna take this anymore!" My thoughts were that I would do all I could to avoid him; I would go a different route if possible.

Going with the flow is fine if you're referring to a river, but not always with life.

But a shift happened in my life shortly afterward. I began to watch an actor on TV named Jean-Claude Van Damme. He became one of my idols. I would watch the movie *Bloodsport*, and then I would try to imitate the moves he'd done during the movie.

My mom saw me flipping around, kicking the air, trying spin moves. She said, "Well, this is pretty cool. Maybe I should get you into martial arts." That was that. She signed me up, and if you're thinking that I took to it like a duck to water, you're wrong! I had a couple of lessons and did begin to feel a sense of empowerment, but along with that came having to do a lot of training work that I just wasn't mentally ready for. I went to karate class three times a week and each class lasted two hours (back in the 90s). I got burned out quickly! I was ready to quit. So I talked to my mom. Her answer was a definitive, "No." Like any good mom, she said, "NO!"

Part of the reason I wanted to quit was because of Nina. Nina was simply a bad-to-the-bone martial artist. She was the best in our class. She was the best looking and had the best punches — she was the total package. Somehow, I always ended up with her as my sparring partner. Now, here's the thing...I was awesome at sparring...until Nina stood in front of me. It deflated me, so I begged my mom to quit. I tried bargaining with her. I told her that I would clean the house and cook gourmet dinners. I was desperate. My mom gave me the final word that I would finish what I started. She told me that I could either walk (we lived about 20 miles away), or I could have her take me. "But the choice is yours," she said. Well, of course, that didn't sound like much of a choice. The rest is history. I am thankful for those moments. I am even thankful for every butt kicking that Nina gave. She was part of the lesson of life for me. Looking back on those moments, I realize that when it comes to "courage," sometimes you need someone else to have it for you until you can summon it within yourself. I always felt a little different. It always seemed like I spent a lot of my life being singled out or just not meeting the criteria of what others thought I needed. I got teased for wearing shoes from the wrong store; they weren't Jordans or some other high-dollar brand. I didn't wear Tommy Hilfiger or Guess. And you know how kids are: when they feel left out, all they want to do is fit in. Maybe I was looking for a feeling of safety, security or approval. Maybe I needed validation to prove that I was worthy enough. It left me feeling lonely, which caused me to shift into a type of daily survival mode. All I wanted to do was survive each day be done, eat dinner, go to bed.

I was enrolled in a private school during part of my elementary school days in Cleveland. Like many private schools, they had a dress code. The boys were all required to wear a tie, and the girls had to wear a skirt. At first, it was a relief to think that I would never have to worry about fitting in again. It was a weight off my shoulders. I could walk proudly down the halls without encountering anyone who was going to call me out based on wearing the wrong thing. Unfortunately, that relief was short-lived because I found out about "dress-down days." Those were special days set aside so that we could wear anything we wanted. For some people, that was what they most looked forward to. For me, it felt like I was right back where I started, singled out in the worst way. I was different, and I just couldn't figure out why. I was somehow able to summon my courage once again to dig deep and make the best of my circumstances.

When it comes to "courage," sometimes you need someone else to have it for you until you can summon it within yourself.

A change came when my family moved to a different part of town, Richmond Heights. The school was multicultural, so for the first time, I felt like I fit in.

My friends were all different races, and they respected me and treated me as an equal. It never mattered what I was wearing, I was accepted. Just as I was getting fully settled in and beginning to feel like this was how the rest of my life would be — awesome — we moved to the little town of Owasso, Oklahoma.

Owasso looks like a totally different town now, compared to when we first moved there. The city has exploded and grown in population over the years! When we moved there though, I had never even visited Oklahoma, and for all I knew, it was still the untamed land of the plains. Just kidding, I seriously didn't think it would be that — but I had no idea what to expect. As I walked through the halls of the school that first time, one thing was obviously different…I rarely saw another black student. I could walk certain areas in the school and I was the only black person. I felt a little bit like I was on display, not necessarily in a bad way (the girls loved my long eyelashes), but I was asked all kinds of ridiculous questions, from my hair to my eyes. I had never seen a Confederate flag until I moved to Oklahoma. Once I learned more about what that stood for, it felt kind of strange that people seemed to be okay with it. I missed my old town, my old school and my friends. Keep in mind, there was no Facebook, Instagram or texting during those days.

Finally, my senior year arrived. It took a while, but I was at a place where I felt like I fit in. Due to the growth, the town and the school were attracting more diversity in the population. It was a beautiful thing because that made it possible for me to have friends of all different races. My school years taught me so much. A lot of those lessons didn't stick with me until I became an adult. But one lesson I learned early on was that I love a variety of cultures and races. That variety allowed me to show up anywhere and be myself.

Some people work so hard at "perfection," they miss the idea of enjoying the journey and the work they put in to get to the top.

Learning to let go of pressure and be myself was the key! I realized as I turned from a kid into a man, that pressure was a part of life. I would add to that, the difference maker is how someone handles pressure. Does it drive you to improve your life or drive you to step away and hide in fear? It takes courage to be a fighter. You have to promote yourself, including selling tickets. That means even if you have to drive here, there and everywhere, you are personally expected to sell them. Why? Because it shows your fans that you care and that you are invested. You are also your brand/business. All the while, you still have to make time to train because most fighters still work a full-time job. There isn't an overwhelming amount of money to be made for just simply fighting.

If you've seen various wrestling leagues, cage fighters and boxing matches on television or streaming live, you've probably heard about the money some of those men and women are collecting. Everyone automatically assumes fighters like me make the big bucks too. Well, unfortunately that just isn't so. If you happen to search my name online, you might see somewhere that I'm worth millions of dollars. This just isn't so. I've had to work hard to sell tickets to fights and do my own promotions. I would love to see my sport gain the notoriety and the payout purse that some of the other sports do, but at the moment, we fight for the love of the battle, not the money.

All of the lessons I learned in school have made me the courageous man I am today. I'm ready to step into the ring of life knowing I overcame bullying, Nina and the task of creating a new version of myself when we moved to Oklahoma. And that allowed me to see myself as a victor, not a victim. That allowed me to bravely step into my new life. As Nelson Mandela said, "I learned that courage was not the absence of fear, but the triumph over it. The brave man is not the one who does not feel afraid, but he who conquers that fear." Some people work so hard at "perfection," they miss the idea of enjoying the journey and the work they put in to get to the top.

Balance is a key that has served me well. For years, I let myself live however I wanted to live, but still expected my body to perform at peak level. That was wrong. When you realize there's a road to follow to your dreams, you have to be aware of the ditch on each side. On one side of the ditch is perfectionism, and on the other side is the temptation to do whatever you want, whenever you want. It takes courage to stay on the path.

ROUND TWO

INTEGRITY

"Real integrity is doing the right thing, knowing that nobody's going to know whether you did it or not." –Oprah Winfrey

I n the fighting world, especially in the world of martial arts, it is about fairness and doing what is right. It's about making decisions in life that you can stand firm with and know you've done the right thing. Integrity may seem obvious when it comes to defining it. However, I want to offer a thought to you that may challenge your definition of integrity. We can probably all agree that integrity has roots in honesty and strong moral principles. But it is also defined as "the state of being whole and undivided; the condition of being unified, unimpaired or sound in construction; internal consistency or lack of corruption (in electrical data)."

The following story will help illustrate a couple of these additional definitions. I've made clear that most of my life I was a fairly humble and non-aggressive kid. It's true. I have lived my adult life in a similar way, though I have a special set of skills that could inflict serious harm to a person, even death. I would never, and have never, set out to use those skills for anything other than inside the kickboxing ring/cage. As a kid, I knew the rules and disciplines of karate that I was learning were strictly to stay inside the class with an instructor present.

Sometimes we're faced with an inescapable moment that forces us to decide what we're going to do.

Now, as you read the following story, you may agree or not with how I chose to deal with what happened. As a father, I understand those of you who feel strongly about not promoting violence of any kind, ever. I also understand those of you who feel otherwise and all of you who are somewhere in between. Since I've grown older, the value of integrity is front and center in everything I do. That is why I'm including this story. When it comes to "the state of being whole and undivided" (part of the integrity definition), the outcome of this story is the truth of where I was at the time. I'm not sugarcoating it or defending it. Telling this story is also not condoning my actions to inspire any reader to imitate or encourage anyone else to imitate my actions. Now, on to the story.

I was never big into trying to prove that I had any kind of "right fight" inside of me when I was young. Life wasn't about proving anything or trying to make people see me and accept me. I coasted with the attitude of "what will be, will be." Sometimes we're faced with an inescapable moment that forces us to decide what we're going to do. Will we take a stand for ourselves, and what does that look like?

For me, that moment came in high school. My senior year in high school was awesome! I had a great group of friends and had built up some muscles to go with my confidence. I was about 5'10" and had been lifting weights off and on. My high school was fairly large, we had 700–800 kids in our graduating class. In spite of the large school, the town was small. Our high school only had a handful of black kids, but I was usually treated very well. Perhaps it was because I carried myself with an air of confidence, but most of the time I didn't have anyone bothering me...until one day I went to open my locker and found a note inside.

As I opened the note, I noticed chicken-scratch racist words with a hangman-style (like the game) drawing that had spaces for the letters of my first and last name:

R _ _ _ _ B _ _ _ _ with the first letters of my name written in. What jarred me at first, was that obviously this person knew my name. After that, notes came every day. They escalated to drawings of Confederate flags, racist jokes, Nazi flags/symbolism and jokes using the N-word.

For those of you wondering if I told the authorities in my school, trust me, I told teachers, and even the principal. Their answers were all the same: "Since you don't know who it is, there's not much we can do." Or: "Just let it slide and move on." Or: "We can't do anything unless we know who is doing it." For months, I would dread going to my locker because I would find another note. Every. Single. Day. The notes attacked my soul. If you haven't ever been attacked for just being "you," for parts of you that represent your identity and your entire being, it might be hard for you to understand why it bothered me so much. But those notes pierced my spirit, and what was worse, is that for a brief period of time I felt alone. Something rose on the inside of me at some point however, and I decided…enough is enough!

I put the word out to my friends, and they were definitely on the lookout and had my back. One day, a buddy of mine overheard some people talking about the notes, and he found out exactly who it was. I will never forget the day my friend ran to me while I was in the lunch line. He was out of breath and panting, and he told me the name of the guy. Here's the kicker: I didn't even know him. However, my friend knew where he lived, so we decided to pay him a visit. I had a few friends with me, and as we pulled up, there were some guys standing out in front of the apartment complex. I asked which of them was Bob. A guy responded to me, and I got in his face and asked why all the notes and all the racial mess…why did he have his sights set on me?

He responded, "Because that's how I was raised; I don't think you belong in our school." My heart dropped with anger. Again, he said, "It's just how I was raised, and I don't like niii—" Before he could get the rest of the word out, I reared back and knocked him smooth out to the ground…one punch. I roared like a lion and asked, "Who else wants some?!" The other three guys with him waved their hands saying "no - no - no." They told me that they had been constantly telling him to stop and that nothing he was doing was funny. That took care of the incidents at school, and the rest of my senior year was peaceful.

More than likely, you're interested in this book because the front photo caught your attention, or you're a sports buff, or maybe the idea of getting inside the mind of a fighter and martial artist interests you. So, let's take a look for a moment at the differences between martial arts (what I do) versus boxing. Sometimes, people tend to group us all together, but we are very different.

What I do is kickboxing, and that is a series of basic punch combinations. There is a form of boxing involved, but you get to throw kicks too. If you've ever seen photos or video of a kickboxing fight, you may have noticed that we wear the same size gloves as boxers. But as I mentioned, we can also strike with our feet. There's no hitting the back of the head…ever. That's in any combat sport. You can't hit the back of the head, back of the neck, or the back in general. You can hit the butt with kicks, or the hamstrings and the calves. Those off-limit back areas that I mentioned are because there's a risk of paralyzation, brain damage and things like that. We're trying to keep the sport as clean as possible, and that requires us to operate with integrity even in our strikes. It sounds brutal (and it is), but I can also throw knees and go outright for the chin. I can knee to the gut but not the groin. Those are some of the technical parts of my sport. Now, let's get into the mental aspects.

Many people take martial arts classes of some sort, at some point in their life. Through my career, I have met many parents who enroll their kids into martial arts because they've been told it will help their focus or help their self-discipline. Of the adults I've met through the years that enroll in classes, most of the time it has been related to health and fitness. Fans who sit in the bleachers or watch a football game from home, yelling at the coach to "run the ball" or "pass the ball," are called armchair quarterbacks. That fan may think they know best, but they haven't put in the years of training, and they have no idea what it's really like out there on the field. Same with my sport.

As a fan, or even someone who takes regular martial arts classes, you might have had the thought, *How hard could it be to really fight?* I have heard it before from people that think they are in excellent condition. They've learned the moves. They've seen the fighters walk down the ramp, dressed in the showy fight trunks. They hear the loud music and the ring announcer belting out the name of the fighters. They see the crowd go wild and then "Ding!" and there's a throwdown!

What could never be shown in the ring/cage are the months of preparation. I could never show you the choices I've had to make when no one else is watching. My determination to live a lifestyle of preparing for victory, not just for one fight, but for all of them, was all about integrity. I knew that although no one was watching if I was in my car and decided to eat a bunch of junk food, or if I slacked off on a workout, I would know, and I was only accountable to myself. Think about how great a NASCAR driver treats their race car. Jeff Gordon was a fierce competitor for NASCAR, and he never put retread tires or the cheapest fuel or oil in his car. If he would have, we would never have known his name because he never would have won. Instead, he put the best tires, the best gas and oil, and did everything possible to treat his machine the best. Then it was up to his training and team to help him win. That's the same for a fighter like me. I put all the best food inside of my body, I read and listen to mentally strong people who say encouraging, positive and motivating words. I practiced to be physically, mentally, emotionally and spiritually strong. Living that way has continued to serve me well to this day.

When I was up for my first World Championship fight, my lifestyle was going to be put to the test. It's an interesting story because I had no clue I was even eligible for a World Championship fight. My opponent, Mike Sheppard, was traveling all around the world, knocking all kinds of bad dudes out, and I mean these were "bad-to-the-bone" dudes. He had pretty much won against everybody in the United States that he faced, making him eligible for another championship bout.

I was an up-and-coming young guy, and at that time, I hadn't lost a fight. Eventually, I became the number one contender. That made me eligible to challenge Mike Sheppard, the current World Champion. I was proud that I also wiped out my competition — everybody in Oklahoma — and even still to this day, I have not lost to one man from Oklahoma, and I've competed in four different weight classes.

There is a ranking system in the fight world. The more you win, the more you move up. If you lose, you go down. And a lot of people in my weight class, from all around the fighting world at that time, would challenge me to fight in order to increase their ranking. So, as the story goes, I crossed paths with Mike Sheppard. He was a guy who beat me in the early days of my fighting career, and he noticed that I was rising through the ranks. This was all part of the Chuck Norris World Combat League in 2008.

He viewed the idea of scheduling a fight with me kind of like a tune-up. In my mind, he was not threatened by me in any form because he had already won against me. I would be just another fight on his way to retain the ISKA World Championship belt. He even made the comment that he was coming to Oklahoma to give me a "spanking," and he was going to "put me in my place just like he would his own son if he got out of line." That didn't intimidate me, in fact it drove me harder. Who knows, Mike may have known that though. He was a smart man and spouting off those comments was like bait for a fish. That's how it all started. But I was not that same guy he fought and won against before.

The fight was set to be held in Oklahoma, and I'm sure Mike probably thought he would humiliate me in front of my home crowd in Tulsa, Oklahoma. It had been four years since our original fight, and a lot had changed in me since that time. Not only was I larger and more solid, I was prepared mentally.

*I was not that same guy he fought
and won against before.*

The Hard Rock Casino hosted the fight. My fans, family and friends showed up to cheer me on. As the bell rang to start the fight, he tried taking my head off. He tried and tried, but I learned to keep the left hand super high because of the technique Mike used to knock his opponents out. It was called "the hammer." Imagine a baseball player, how they wind up to throw a pitch that ends up being a curveball. The pitch looks normal, but the ball makes a curve at the last minute to cause the batter to swing, and hopefully for the pitcher, miss. That's how Mike would do it: he would throw his fist, but it wouldn't come straight at you, it would loop around and catch you and lay you flat out!

I was able to deter him from landing "the hammer" on me. With a flying knee to Mike's face, the fight was over. Winning that night was a great lesson for me in understanding that sometimes we have to be persistent in our pursuit of winning.

Here's an interesting fact about that evening. It took place in Tulsa, Oklahoma, on June 1, 2012. Decades before my fight night, another fight took place in Tulsa: from May 31 – June 1 of 1921 (91 years prior), the city of Tulsa looked very different from my night of celebration. An area known as "Black Wall Street" was burning. Following World War I, Tulsa had a thriving and affluent African American community known as the Greenwood District. The spark of the massacre took place when a young black man named Dick Rowland was arrested following an accusation from a young white woman named Sarah Page. Sadly, many of the African American community were injured or killed. You can learn more about the event from various websites, such as www.tulsahistory.org, www.okhistory.org, and many others. It was not required to teach this part of Oklahoma's history until after I graduated high school. The Tulsa Race Massacre gained national attention during the 100th anniversary, and that is when I began to put the facts together about the significance of my fight date.

As a young black man, I am so proud to have represented the black community by winning the World Championship and standing in the city 91 years later in victory, instead of defeat.

ROUND THREE

PERSEVERANCE

"Great things come from hard work
and perseverance. No excuses."
—Kobe Bryant

Perseverance is a key to being successful in whatever it is that you do. But being honest with yourself is also key. I've learned through fighting, that heavy training is involved in order to achieve greatness, two to three times a day, every day. Diet, recovery, no sex and no partying/clubbing are all components that have helped with that. If any of these are lacking, then it will show up during fight night. There is no one to blame but yourself. That is why perseverance starts before the match. It starts months before a ticket is ever sold. Persevering and completing everything on the (component) list is what makes a winner.

After I graduated from high school, I felt lost. It had taken me such a long time to get to the place where I was finally comfortable with who I was. I finally fit in and had my own circle of friends. All of that dissipated to some degree after graduation. Now I know, that was all a natural part of life's progression. Most of the time after graduation, kids are moving off to colleges around the country and making major changes to follow their dreams. I had dreams too, but really had no certainty about the direction I should go. I wasn't focused on how to make my dreams of possibly playing in the NBA a reality. My life lacked a lot of discipline and direction. Sometimes, a young person needs someone to believe in them and to call out their greatness. My parents definitely believed in me, but their thoughts were always corporate or business life. At that time, I just couldn't see that being my path. So, where would I go and what was I put on this earth to achieve? Those thoughts nagged at me. I wanted to make a difference and little did I know, but the doors were about to open for me to do just that.

As I searched for what I would do in life, I decided

I would give college a go. My dream was to play in the NBA and to be like Mike! Michael Jordan. I traveled around the US to a few colleges with my dad in hopes of landing a scholarship. With nothing set in stone, I ended up at a junior college in the middle of nowhere — Seminole, Oklahoma. I was able to be a "walk on" for the team. That meant no financial aid, no athletic scholarship. They were offering me an opportunity to show what I could do first, and then they'd consider where to go from there. After a year of that, I dropped out. I was not motivated and had no desire to continue.

Discouraged, I went back to live with my parents. That was the point I began walking down a dark path, lost with no direction. Feeling like that certainly made me susceptible to an undisciplined lifestyle. There was very little routine, other than my job as a bouncer, but fortunately, part of my routine still included regular karate classes. But I was not competing, and it was the furthest thing from my mind.

One of my instructors was named David "Master Kick" Vogtman. He taught karate, and I loved his class. One day, he told me that he was teaching a fighting class, and he thought I might be good enough to join it. My response…"Cool." Then David told me, "Well, you have to be invited, you can't just join on your own. And I'm the one who decides who gets invited." When David said, "Man, you know what? It's time you come and try the fight class out." When I asked why, he told me, "When you spar people, you have to learn control. You can't have people getting knocked out in class or ending up with a broken nose or something like that. You need to see what it feels like to hit somebody." He continued, "I'm not asking you to be a fighter. But unlike the karate sparring class where it's an accident if someone hits you too hard, the fight class is where someone can hit you hard and you can hit back!" I said, "Okay, I think I might want to give that a shot!"

So, I ended up trying the fighter class. I really enjoyed it and it didn't stop there. One day, in the other sparring class, David was there and told me, "Randy, you got it dude. I think you should be a fighter. I think you should pursue it. You can do a lot of things in life, but I think you should get in the ring. Knocking somebody out is going to be one of the best feelings you could imagine. You've got what it takes to be a champion." Keep in mind, I was only about 19 years old. *Champion? How on earth am I going to be a champion?*

Although I couldn't see myself as a fighter or a

champion, I decided to attend a few local fights to check out what the true experience might be like. I wanted to see it firsthand. What did it look like? What was the crowd reaction? What was the atmosphere? All those things were part of what I wanted to see firsthand. I was still attending and training in the fight class. I just wasn't "hungry," and I wasn't honest about where I was in life. I wanted to be liked and respected, but I wasn't telling the truth to myself about what I needed to change in order to get to that place. My job at the time was as a bouncer in a club. It was kind of cool because I could handle situations and people if they got crazy. But I was staying out till 4:00 or 5:00 in the morning, sleeping during the day, and my diet was terrible.

Considering how much goes into preparing for a fight, that lifestyle was not going to work. I knew I couldn't be at the club every weekend ingesting smoke and being around alcohol and all the other nonsense that went on. Looking back, it was weird that I chose that job because I didn't drink or smoke. I haven't ever done drugs, but I was always around other people who did. It was my way of fitting in I suppose, trying to seek other people's approval. It's interesting how much one person can impact your life.

Without that original conversation with David Vogtman, I don't think you'd be reading a book with my name on it. There wouldn't have been a championship, a fight, a fighter's class, or anything for me to share with people about what I've learned in my life. He shed light on something inside me when he told me the power of channeling my drive into a fighter's path. David told me that power and drive were only reserved for a few who were willing to leave "normal" behind and go for excellence. He did not candy-coat the idea that I was about to step into something that would challenge me in a way I had never experienced before. He laid the challenge out and asked me if I was ready for it, and with that challenge, I said, "Yes!"

---

*It's interesting how much one person
can impact your life.*

All of that was a turning point in my life. Here's a powerful thought...after that time, I never saw that man again. So, you never know what impact your words to encourage or direct something you see in someone else might have on them. When I entered into the fighting class, I began to change my life, and that set me on the path I'm on today. I had to see myself for who I was in order to begin to make the changes and live honestly. Honesty, for me, is not only telling the truth to others, but it's also telling myself the truth.

Once I began the fighting class, I kept it to myself. I didn't want my mom to be worried about me getting hurt, and I wasn't sure how far I was going in the early days.

I was training in fighting class regularly, and my coach at the time was Mike Eagan. I longed for his approval. He would give constant attention to other fighters, and although I was the new guy, I just wanted some kind of "atta-boy" from him. He'd cross his arms and watch. For all the coaches and athletes here: it's your coach's job to give all of his undivided attention to the class/team. You are in a relationship with that person(s), and they want to see you pay your dues. One day, after about a month, Mike came over and walked up to my right ear and said, "Turn your right shoulder." Then he walked off. I froze. I turned my right shoulder and kept training.

Periodically, over the weeks, he would come over

and talk to me more and more. Finally, I worked myself up to where I got my fight. My first fight. So now, I would have to tell my mom.

Me: "Mom, guess what?"

Her: "What's up?"

Me: "You know all those fights that we used to go to? The local fights?"

Her: "Yeah."

Me: "I get to be in one this weekend."

Her: "What?! No! What are you talking about?"

Me: "This will be great! It's a great opportunity!"

Her: "Out of all the things you could be in this world, you want to go jump in the ring and let some grown man beat you? Beat up on you? Hurt my baby."

Me: "Mom, I'm not a baby."

Dad jumps in: "Yeah, I watched Mike Tyson and all kinds of fights, now I have a reason to go watch and support somebody live." So, I made my way through that conversation and went forward.

I was full of attitude because I was determined to come out on top.

My mother loved me, and of course, her words were not to discourage me in following my dream, but to protect me. So, how did it all turn out from her perspective after that conversation? My mom actually started her own martial-arts journey when I was in college. Today, she is a two-time World Champion in BJJ (Brazilian Jiu Jitsu) through Master Carlos Machado. She is also the first female in Oklahoma to achieve Black Belt status in BJJ. So, that says it all! I'm so proud of my amazing mom!

I'm sure any athlete can probably identify with the shift in focus that happens with the type of training needed for competition, as opposed to training in general. You have to make a mental shift. When it came to fighting, obviously I wasn't going to walk in downtown Tulsa and deck someone if they looked at me sideways. There's a fight mode, but it doesn't apply to everyday life. That's why I mentioned that you'd never know I was a kickboxer and could do some serious damage to you. That's something only reserved for the ring.

Inside the ring — or whatever your mode of competition might be; a court, a courtroom, a field, a stage or wherever your "fight mode" happens to be — is reserved for that special space. For me, that was the ring. Inside the ring, I was selfish; I wasn't going to submit; I was full of attitude because I was determined to come out on top.

But I knew, that person had to stay *inside* the ring/cage because no one wants *that* man in their life on a daily basis. Hey, I had about 25 minutes in me for the fight…after that, I want to relax!

Fight night arrived. I was young and just learning to fight. That first professional fight was lackluster, to say the least. When you see movies about how the fighters have these big locker-room atmospheres and a sea of people in the audience to watch, they make it look kind of glamorous. Add to that, in the movies they make it seem like hundreds of thousands of dollars are on the line. But here's the reality from my first experiences. The "locker rooms" stunk — literally. There were dumpy little rooms that had no toilets; sometimes, we changed in the kitchen in the back room of the venue. The crowd may have numbered about 300 on a good night! Did I rake in hundreds of thousands, even thousands of dollars, during those days? No! In fact, my first fight I was to make $90, but they ended up adding a bonus, and I brought home $100. Don't get me wrong, I'm actually not complaining. Those were the days of paying my dues. I learned so much during those early times. It helped to make me the man I am today. When someone complains about having to work their way up, whether it's in martial arts or any other career, they don't get sympathy from me. Instead, I offer understanding. I know what it's like to face the hardships of just starting out. I know how hard it is to prove yourself and how much you'll question yourself. Starting out, it may be obvious that you have talent to do what you're pursuing, but that voice inside can sure try to make you believe that you are an imposter. That inside voice also may try to tell you that it's never going to work, and you're never going to make it past the starting point. But don't give up! Persevere through the tough times and the criticism, even if you're the worst critic of yourself. No one starts as the best at anything. In fact, there's a statistic that says it takes up to 10,000 hours to master anything. That equals a little over a year of practice. I'm not saying that's an exact science, but it definitely has a ring of truth to it. If you think about any famous musician, athlete or comedian, I imagine they would tell you that they've spent at least a year to hone their gift. When you have spent all those hours and years practicing, then there's room for you when that moment comes and you get your big break.

Think about NFL quarterback Tom Brady. Whether you like him or not, the facts don't lie. He began as a backup quarterback for Drew Bledsoe. Drew got hurt, and the coach used Tom as his replacement. Now, he's a seven-time Super Bowl winner, and many call him the GOAT (Greatest of all time).

Persevere through the tough times and the criticism, even if you're the worst critic of yourself.

We all have our beginnings. Only a few people get an opportunity like Tom Brady. My opportunity came with a fight in the Chuck Norris World Combat League when I was only supposed to be there as an alternate, basically in a learning capacity. I was technically on the team, but I wasn't supposed to fight.

Out of all the times in my life up unto this point, this moment I felt like I didn't fit in more than ever before. I had competed in a total of three fights up to this point, but nothing on this level.

The other competitors were well known and well respected. This league was all World Champions.

Not me. As far as I was concerned, I was there to watch and learn for my debut the next season.

The concept of this league was unique from how kickboxing is, so let me explain how the rules work. Every person on the team is matched to fight a person from the other team.

Each teammate earns points towards the team total. Every person on the team is matched to fight a person from the other team. Our team was the Oklahoma Destroyers and we were matched against a team from Texas called The Texas Dragons. World Combat League athletes are well-conditioned, exciting professional CMA (Combat Martial Arts) fighters. In an effort to encourage consistent "full-throttle" fighting action, each athlete is required to compete in two three-minute fights with a significant rest period in between. It's exactly what it sounds like: all-out, pedal to the metal, boom-boom-boom type of fighting. In fact, any attempt to stall or fight passively is penalized. This also allows for exciting fights to happen, one after another.

At the end of each fight, the judges' scores are announced and added to a cumulative total for the team. After each team member has fought, there is a halftime. That is when the coaches work on strategy.

The team that has the most cumulative points when the final fight is concluded is crowned the winner. That gives you a little insight into why it's so important for each team member to carry their weight and do their best.

A guy from our team in my weight class was fighting, and the match was going back and forth. The round ended in a draw, and as I watched, my thought was that *surely our guy will win the next round.* The dude from my team (whom we are going to call Bob) came back to the locker room at halftime and he yelled, "Oh man, my shoulder, my shoulder! I can't move it! I felt it pop out!"

The coaches yelled back at him, "Hey, you got to get back out there. I don't care if you lose or if you get knocked out, but you're getting back out there!"

Now he was begging, "I can't do it, I just can't! Please! Please, I'm begging you, please, please, please, please. I'm not going back out there." That guy's pride and lack of perseverance could have cost the team a victory.

The coaches came over to me and said, "Randy, sorry man, I hate to do this to you." I knew what was coming. Interestingly, I was dressed out as if I would be fighting but had no plans to, as I already stated. My coach was trying to console me before he presented what was about to happen. I thought to myself, *Ahhh yes*. It was like an inner-child moment. "Randy, I don't have a choice. Look, I just want you to know I love you, and you'll always be on the team. You'll always be with us. You'll always be one of my Black Belts." That was Dale "Apollo" Cook talking, by the way. He was one of the coaches. He was saying things like," Just use your reach." At that moment, we all had so much going on in our minds. I'm sure he probably thought, *Man, what do I say to this kid?* But I was at a place, mentally and physically, where I knew I was ready.

At that point, I was always having to prove myself. I hadn't really convinced anyone that I was good fighting material. This moment was an opportunity to show that all the time, training and attention from the coaches would pay off. This would be my introduction into the World Combat League — trial by fire, so to speak.

My opponent was a killer and had won a lot of fights. I got out there with him. He had never been knocked out before. He had so many advantages at that moment. I was the new guy, the young guy. Nobody knew my name except my parents. I made it to the team with two amateur fights and one pro fight. I got out there, and we were moving around… suddenly, I knew it was time. I dropped him with a spinning back kick! He got back up and I hit him again. He was done! That's actually how I got my nickname, Boom! Boom!

I took him out with two hard knocks to the solar plexus. Chuck Norris was there that night, and he waved at me and bowed. My mind was spinning like my back kick: *Wow, man this was so cool. I just fought in front of freaking Chuck Norris!* Keep in mind that sometimes others see something inside of you way before you see it in yourself.

If someone calls you beautiful (YES! YOU… reading this book!), you may not see yourself as beautiful, but you are. I'm telling you, you look great and you are amazing. You may not see it yet, but I do, or someone else does. That was the same feeling I had. There was no way in my mind I could knock anyone out at all, much less be the World Champion! When opportunities come to test our endurance, it's then we see whether we will persevere and turn a trial into a triumph.

My trial came in the form of a physical injury that I suffered the day before a "fight day."

One afternoon, I was driving my car, minding my

own business, when…Wham! I was broadsided on the driver's side. Airbags deployed, my ribs hit the middle console and all of me slammed toward the right side. Honestly, I thought my nose was broken by the force of the airbag. Yet, I didn't have any bruises or broken bones. My OnStar went off, and a voice came over the speakers: "Mr. Blake, are you okay? Are you responsive? Are you okay?"

And I told them, "Yeah, I'm fine…I was hit." (That gave my condition away didn't it? I was obviously stunned but not seriously hurt.)

"Yeah, we know, Mr. Blake, that's why we're calling you." Keep in mind, this is the middle of June in Oklahoma. Hot. I got out of my car a little woozy and went to check on the person who hit me. She was an older lady driving an older car, and get this, her vehicle barely had a scratch on it. We waited for the police to arrive and take down a report.

About thirty minutes into this car accident scene, my arm was on fire. I mean F-I-R-E. Initially, I thought it was probably because of the jolting and the debris from the airbag. The paramedic poured water on my arm when I mentioned the pain. But due to whatever chemical is inside the air bag, that water seemed to be like cracking an egg on a 115-degree sidewalk in

Oklahoma in the summer...sizzling hot. All the time we were outside, I was sweating and feeling terrible. And then it hit me...

I have to weigh in for my fight tomorrow, and I probably just shed 10 pounds.

Weigh-ins, for fighters, are an opportunity to build confidence. It's a mental match before the physical match. You've probably seen the fighters or boxers who scowl and look all tough when they step onto the scale before their match. They stare down their opponent and try to make them react. Fighters are always looking for anything to turn into "an angle" they can use before and during the fight.

Well, I certainly wasn't going to tell anyone or let the word get out about my car accident. I knew that would get into my head and would certainly be a boon to my opponent's head. It would be like spilling a bucket of chum into shark-infested waters — the frenzy would be on.

So, here were the variables...

1. I was in terrible pain. My arm felt like it was literally on fire.
2. I'd sold so many tickets. I knew I would have an awesome home crowd.
3. I couldn't let those people down.

I did my best to sleep it off that night and head to the weigh-in that next morning. I played off any hint of injury. I certainly wasn't going to tell the trainer or medical personnel anything. Before each fight, in addition to weighing, you have a routine physical that assesses if you're really able to fight. They have you do a series of push-ups, duck walks (close to floor squatting while you walk) and squats. They check your knuckles and they push on the sides of your ribs. Does it make you hurt just reading that last part? Yeah, me too.

By that morning, I was feeling all the pain left over from the accident. That's how it usually happens, but most people aren't about to enter a fight ring where someone will be doing their best to punch and kick you right in the ribs.

When opportunities come to test our endurance,
it's then we see whether we will persevere
and turn a trial into a triumph.

Because I knew it was coming, I held my breath and closed my eyes to focus. I told myself, *You got this.*

I couldn't wince, or they would have called the fight. There wasn't any way in the world I was going to let my opponent beat me, by forfeit or otherwise.

Fight night arrived, and I went after him hard. Watch the film, and you'd never know I had been in a car accident. I won that fight by a knockout. I finished the dude! After the fight, when I was handed the mic, I told the story about the accident, and people were freaking out. "Why are you here?" was the common question I was asked after the fight that night. My answer to that question now: When you understand how to persevere, you keep going until it becomes ingrained in you.

"Never, never, never give up." Winston Churchill. Although that quote is attributed to Winston Churchill, I know we've all heard it said by various people in our lives. Sometimes, we have had to learn to say it to ourselves. That thought is what kept me moving, training and preparing myself through all circumstances to overcome and win. If you watch an Olympian, they train for years to perform a few minutes during the actual competition. But that athlete is at their peak condition, and if they aren't allowed to compete for some reason, it's like starting all over again. In my case, I'm consistent with my workouts. But when I'm preparing for a fight, there is much more intense training that is added to my typical routine. If a fight is delayed or canceled, I have months to wait until my next one can be scheduled. That is the value of preparation, and it should give you insight into why I'm willing to push through and persevere through difficult circumstances. And although it was difficult to push through the pain in my ribs after the car accident, nothing could have prepared me for what I was about to face.

I was training to fight a guy from Great Britain named Aundre Groce. This was 2016, and it was for the ISKA World Heavyweight Title. I had been watching all kinds of films of his fights. That's a preparation that many competitive athletes do. When you watch what your competition does, it gets you familiar with their moves. For me, that helped me feel like I understood him and his method of fighting. Interesting note: in the fighting world, as you win, you increase your rank. As your rank increases, you fight tougher opponents, which is great because it sets up a type of tactical chess match. You don't just run in swinging, hoping to land a punch. Additionally, you don't just start kicking and spinning, hoping to land a kick. No, your opponents will now be just as skilled as you. He's taking life as seriously as you. He's making sacrifices too.

With that in mind, I learned that my goal would be to attack with combinations and an arsenal of kicks. My resources, when it came to kicks, included a wide variety. I'm not one-sided, I can throw the same kicks with both legs. I knew it would have to be mainly my left hook because I noticed something about his right hand when he wasn't kicking: it was always down. So I drilled countless hours of left hook center attacks. I'm left handed by the way, so it built extra confidence in me to land that shot.

Fight night. We met in the center of the ring before the opening bell to do our stare-down. I winked at him and smiled. Remember at the beginning, I said that if I walked into where you were that you'd never guess I was a fighter? Although true, when I'm in the ring, you'd never guess I was a nice guy. Outside the cage, or ring, I'm chill. Let's go get something to eat, let's watch TV, let's have fun. Inside the cage, it's about winning. Today is not going to be your day. That's my mentality, and that's how I walk into the ring. You have to be a little bit selfish inside the ring, or the bell on the floor isn't the only thing that will get rung, your head will too.

At the World Championship level, you take any advantage you can. So, when I winked at him, it was my way of telling him, "You're in my hometown now, this is my world title, and it's staying here in Tulsa."

Another tactical advantage when I was fighting at home was to get my students involved. When I would make my way down the ramp from behind the curtain, I had every student whose parents purchased tickets come down with me. It gave me the home advantage. Usually, there would be anywhere from 20–50 kids, ranging from age 4 to 17, marching down that ramp. We were all going to war. I loved to have those kids feel the rush of walking down with the music blaring, the crowd going wild. That was me at my absolute peak. The energy from the kids was fuel for me.

They even got to see their instructor at his best and his worst. My best was my peak condition, my worst was being injured after a wreck and when I tore my bicep. This is what I truly believe makes a World Champion of any sort of sport. At the end of the day, I'm human. I have flaws. I'm not perfect by any means. In fact, there are many World Champions I could name that far exceeded what I accomplished. Sometimes, however, it is about demonstrating heroism in a way that wasn't planned. I could've used the same excuse/reason Bob from the Oklahoma Destroyers used when he hurt his arm and quit. I chose to take a different path and get back out there and fight with what I had left in the tool box, and victory prevailed through perseverance.

Now back to the fight...bell rings: We move around. I'm scoring points, hurting him. I'm doing everything that I have trained, it's going great. Next, we got into a particular clinch, where I simply put one arm around one side of his neck and my other arm around the other side of his neck. My plan was to shoot a knee. Now...in my version, and in my eyes, I hit a knee shot in his stomach, but he went back and grabbed his groin area. The referee jumped in and called time-out.

I chose to take a different path and get back out there and fight with what I had left in the tool box, and victory prevailed through perseverance.

Side note: when a fighter gets hit in the groin, he has up to five minutes to recover. Most fighters don't take the full five because they want to keep the momentum going. It does sting a bit though, and hopefully, someday, there will be better protection down there.

Back to the fight: I went to a neutral corner, and when I looked down at my arm, my bicep was rolled all the way up underneath my armpit. Strangely, it wasn't until I saw it that the pain kicked in. It was the most excruciating pain that I have ever experienced in my life, even to this day. I hadn't seen it until then because standing there in that neutral corner was the first break in the action since the injury occurred.

That was round 1. Keep in mind, we have one minute between rounds, so these conversations were short and to the point. Now, here's something that I need to interject because it will make sense here...I'm a prankster. I love to play jokes and have fun. Anyone who has been around me very long knows this, so sometimes people don't take me too seriously, including my coach, Peppe Johnson. So, after I realized what happened, I tried to secretly tell my coach. I whispered in a panic, "Coach, I think I broke my arm!"

He responded, "Man, quit playin' — stop it — this is the World (Championship)!" He was mad because he thought I was playing a prank.

"No! Coach! Seriously — my arm!"

And he looked to see my bicep dangling…and he said, "Well you got about 15 seconds left in the round so just move around." So that's what I did, until the bell rang. I had never seen my coaches run into the cage so fast in my life. Usually, they moved slow, it was kind of another mental game to play with the opponent, like, I didn't really need anything from the coaches…just support. But not that night.

As we sat in the corner, my coach said, "What did you do?" I had no idea what or how it happened. I didn't feel a pop, snap, no nothing. So, he was panicking but tried to show me he wasn't panicking… but I definitely knew he was freaking out…and I was too. To top things off, it was my left arm, the one I had been training extra with for this fight. As the next round was about to start, my coach said, "Well, let's see if you can still fight. Go out there and throw some kicks. Throw that right arm if you can — throw it! If you can throw the left, throw it!"

I said, "All right, I got this!" At the bell, I flew out confident. How? I have no idea. But the fight was still in me. It faded a little bit though because the weirdest thing happened with that injury. When I tried to throw my left hand (and arm), the bicep would contract, and it would cause my arm to do the opposite of what I wanted. So, if I threw it *up*, it would go *down*. If I threw it *down*, it would go *up*. I realized that I was going to have to work to control my arm. That was going to change my entire strategy for the fight.

Here's a quick explanation of what happened: I actually ruptured my bicep tendon at the distal end (at the elbow). I lost the ability to pronate (rotate my arm). Because of that, I lost the ability to make a left hook. I realized I would have to just try to slide my arm up to keep it in place. I was in pain beyond belief, and I was so irritated at the same time. I decided to throw my right arm, but it hurt just as bad because the pain was shooting all through both arms by that time. I tried a kick, and that also wasn't working well because of the pain. I started to lose confidence and lose hope.

Round three: Same results. Nothing much happened during that round. Like, nothing. By then, my coach was yelling at me, cussing, "G&* D@#$ it, if you don't throw anything, you're going to lose this fight!

I know we trained for that left hook, but you got so many other skills to use to beat this guy! We may not knock him out tonight, but life isn't about that! It's not about knocking the guy out all the time. Figure out how to unlock the door where he's vulnerable in some other way. But you got to throw something! You got to! Two more rounds…stick with me! That belt (championship belt) is about to go back on that plane with that guy all the way to Great Britain! Is that what you want?! IS THAT WHAT YOU WANT?!!"

That pep talk woke me back up. I felt like Rocky! The conversation intensely affected me — it went inside me. Even as I write this, I get chills thinking about it. When my coach said, "That belt is about to go back on that plane with that guy all the way to Great Britain! IS THAT WHAT YOU WANT?!!" I got so fired up that when the bell rang for round four, I came out firing! I dropped the guy!

---

*…if you don't throw anything, you're
going to lose this fight!*

After I dropped him, he got back up and the crowd went crazy. Keep in mind, up to that point, I could feel the energy from the crowd. It was like they knew something was happening, something was wrong. So now, they were back in it.

At the end of the fight, I got my hand raised, and the crowd went crazy! I retained the belt! There is always a post-fight interview, and I told the crowd it was a tough fight, in fact, one of the toughest fights ever. I told them I was going to have to get my arm checked because something happened during the fight. I showed the crowd, and their gasp told me they knew at that moment why I was "off" during the fight. But their support was awesome and held me together mentally until the fight was completely finished. You could say, we persevered together.

After a fight, there is always a post-fight checkup to make sure there are no broken bones in your face or things like that. If there are, the doctor is required to send you to the hospital. As the doctor was checking me, he told me that he saw my bicep roll up and saw it going up and down. "You got a tear in the distal end." I had no idea what that meant, so he explained, "Basically, your bicep tendon tore. Your bicep is held together by two tendons: the long head, which is up toward the top, and the other end is by the elbow. You tore it in the worst possible spot. You must have surgery, or it could end up frozen in place." The kicker was when he told me that it had to be done within two weeks.

After the fight, I was miserable. I couldn't even pick up my cell phone without my arm totally freezing up in agony. I was thrilled to have won the world title bout, but this definitely was a cloud over the sunshine of that experience. I had proven to myself that I could overcome the biggest obstacle I had faced up to that point. And I won. So now, I was a little over a week into the afterglow of the win and decided to have surgery. It went perfectly, and I was in a soft cast for about two weeks. My doctor told me that I would start physical therapy after that week was over. I was thinking it would last a few weeks, maybe a couple of months. I asked him how long it was going to take because I needed to get ready for my next fight. His answer? "Possibly up to a year."

I was devastated and told him there's no way I could wait a year. He clarified that since I was an athlete in peak condition, that I had a great chance to get back on my feet. I was hoping to start regaining strength overall, but it would be several months before I could use that left arm. Diet, physical therapy and my mental mindset were the parts of the recovery program he emphasized. "It's totally on you," is what he told me. It would be largely mental, not simply physical.

Funny, how you can seem so ready to jump in for the challenge and then feel like you've hit rock bottom. Up until the time I began physical therapy, I was feeling on top of my game mentally. My first visit rolled around and it hit me…in just those two weeks, my arm was already looking skinny. In fact, I had lost all strength in it. I couldn't even lift two pounds — talk about being embarrassed… Here I was, mister macho, built, strong man, and I felt like a weakling. I was weak in that arm and in my mind at that moment.

When someone enters your life at just the right moment to help set you on a positive trail, that person is a gift. Well, my physical therapist was a gift to me. He said, "Yo, we're going to work on this thing, and over time, it'll come back." I couldn't see it yet, but he always believed in me and knew I would catch hold of it. Healing in any form is a process. It takes time.

At that time in my life, it was like I went back to my white belt. The white belt is the first belt, for a beginner in martial arts. I had to go back to basics and relearn how to use my left arm. My physical therapist said, "Every single day we're going to come up here. We're going to do this." He reminded me to eat healthy foods, and he told me I had to take a break from teaching classes for a while. I was a martial arts instructor at the time, and he knew if I was in the classes, working with the kids, that I would be too tempted to play around with the kids. If I wanted to fight again, he told me I had one shot to get this right. And I took it.

Healing in any form is a process. It takes time.

One of the hardest things for me to do during my recuperation was to stay away from the gym. My nature was to keep going, and I loved being in the gym. But I knew he was right. So I kept away. I share that because if I wouldn't have listened to that man, I probably wouldn't be in this position today.

If you've ever been a public figure in your world in any form, you understand how difficult it is to stay away. For example, if you are well known in the motivational speaking world, and you damage your voice in some way and now have to stay away from public speaking, how hard would that be to virtually disappear from your world that you give to and receive from? That is what I faced during that time in my life. Kickboxing wasn't just about the fights, it was my life to be connected to the kids and the families involved in the gym. I was investing in their lives daily, and in an instant, everything changed. Isolation in the sports world means you lose fans and friends.

Out-of-sight, out-of-mind: that's how life felt for me during that time. I know people weren't intentionally forgetting, some of that was just the natural consequence. But the pain of isolation was real, and at times, far outweighed the pain of my physical recovery. I want you to know that if you've ever battled depression or anxiety, I feel you. I understand, and I know the struggle. Don't give up and think there's no light at the end of the tunnel. There is always hope… but I get it. When horrible things have happened, it's really hard to bounce back. Thoughts are the biggest battle. It has been called "the battlefield of the mind" before, and it's true. Our minds are the biggest battlefield, and mine kept lying to me, telling me that I didn't matter anymore. My mind told me that I should just figure out some other life because my career was over. My mind told me that I was never as good as I thought I was in the first place. All of those lies kept me hostage to a shrinking world that I wasn't sure I could climb out of. I had to battle the fear of never being in the kickboxing world again.

Around that time, as I was recouping, something very ironic happened. I was inducted into the USA Martial Arts Hall of Fame. Here I was, not even fighting, and yet they wanted to honor me. Even though that was a huge achievement to have at such a young age (I was 30), I couldn't really enjoy it. I was a World Champion on the one hand, but on the other hand, I couldn't shake the pain that was inside of me.

During that point in my life, it seemed like one hardship happened after the other. Picture dominoes positioned so that when one falls, it lands on the next one and the next, knocking down a row, one after the other. That is how life felt for me.

First domino was that fight which caused me to need surgery and use my fighter's insurance, which ended up in a lawsuit. That was more stressful than I could ever convey here. The worst mental and emotional pain came from that lawsuit. I choose not to air my dirty laundry (because, thankfully, it turned out well overall), but at the time, my entire career and livelihood was on the line. It could have ruined me financially. (That lawsuit experience could have counted for a room full of dominoes.) Next domino was that both of my grandmothers passed away within a short time of each other.

I sunk into a deep depression. I was losing weight and staying up all night because I was unable to sleep. For almost two years, every single night, I would sweat when I was trying to sleep. It didn't matter if I turned the air-conditioning on, or put a fan by my face, I would wake up in a pool of sweat. I was stressed out beyond anything I had ever encountered. That all lasted about four years. It felt like an eternity. Remember, no matter how put-together someone looks on the outside, and no matter how great their life seems to be, you have no idea what battles they face inside. I was proof of that. There has to be a point where you interrupt those thoughts. You have to begin to tell yourself that you are not here by accident. Remind yourself that your life has a purpose, and there is a plan for your life. Whether you believe in God or not, there is more to life than living for yourself. Life for me has to be about my daughter and family and about others. When you take a moment to look outside of the pain you're in and see someone else, help someone else, your life can change. I'm proof you can persevere…never give up, never, never give up!

ROUND FOUR

RESPECT

"I always have tried to treat people with respect,
the way I want to be treated."
-Derek Jeter

What does it feel like when I hit someone? What may seem an odd way to start a section on "respect," is actually perfect. Think about this, I've been trained through martial arts on the value of respect. That means, as you read previously, I am trained to my core that showing value to the life of someone else is paramount. I am also trained that as I show that value to someone else, it becomes ingrained inside of me to show that same respect to myself. So, back to what it feels like when I hit someone. It's a paradox, because on the one hand, it feels great, but on the other hand, I am simply trying to finish the fight, not finish the man.

When someone asked me what it *literally* feels like to make contact with someone in a fight, I explained that there is a sense of euphoria. You see an immediate response in some way, whether they show pain or make a noise. Depending on where you hit the person, there is acute awareness and sensantionon your own skin. For example, hitting the forehead feels like a concrete wall. Strange right? When you kick, sometimes it can feel like you've kicked a branch from a tree. Gut shots near the ribs feels like a waterbed or a leather bag full of water — pliable, but very tough. Sometimes, during the fight, there isn't any awareness/sensation — I'm too focused on the moment, landing strikes and moving to the next and the next and the next. In spite of a fighter's goal to win, at the end of the day, we still respect our opponent's value and the work he has put in to have arrived at this place. I value myself for the same reasons.

A story I love to share is about a guy I fought in 2014, a fighter by the name of Joe Yager. I knew nothing of him at the time. We battled back and forth, and I ultimately came out with the victory. One part of this experience that I remember to this day is when Joe stuck out his hand to shake mine. He said, "It was an honor to fight you; I respect you more than you know homie." That made me smile. Joe invited me to be featured on a TV series that he had going on called, *Zombies Go Boom.* We took turns striking a blood-filled artificial skull that looked like a zombie. A couple of months later, Joe invited me out to train with him and all of his guys. I stayed in his house, and he even gave me a car to drive while I was there. To this day, Joe and I are like brothers. It all began with respect.

After winning my first World Title through ISKA in 2012, I was heavily recruited by one of the biggest organizations kickboxing has ever produced, K-1. This league is considered to be an honor to compete in. Champions like Andy Hug and Ernesto Hoost have competed in K-1, just to name a few.

I can remember staying up late during high school to watch kickboxing on ESPN2. They had two portions to the TV show. The first portion of the show featured martial artists, who competed all over the world in different categories, doing katas, weapons katas and power board-break techniques. Then they shifted it over for the next hour, showing kickboxing fights. These events that were televised were held in Vegas. I remember a particular card where Rick "The Jet" Roufus, a pioneer in the sport of kickboxing, and a guy by the name of Dewey "The Black Kobra" Cooper fought. It happened to be a ISKA-sanctioned fight. I was watching something I had no idea I'd be invested in, years later. Interesting how life comes full circle like that.

Needless to say, I accepted the call from K-1, and this was definitely a step up, as I would be competing against more top-tier competition. My first opponent in K-1 ended up being the man that I stayed up to watch on ESPN2, twice a week. You guessed right, two-time World Champion, Dewey Cooper. Rick Roufus fought that night too, and it was an honor to be on a card with guys who have helped pave the way in top-level kickboxing.

Being a part of that league let me know how far I had truly grown, not only as a martial artist, but as a fighter, athlete and individual.

Looking back, I could remember the early fighting venues: the 300 people I fought in front of, the locker rooms and how they smelled, the toilets that didn't work and so on. Yep, this felt like a brand-new adventure, and I loved it.

The venue we were scheduled to fight in was the Los Angeles Memorial Sports Arena. Once I walked back to the locker room, I was in total awe. I had my own personal room! I had a flatscreen TV that allowed me to keep track of the other fights (helpful in knowing when I needed to be ready — "on deck"). I had fruit, water bottles, showers, a stretching area and toilets with tons of toilet paper.

I know every fighter has experienced this, but it's worth mentioning the "bubble guts." Nervous gut runs. I was nervous like that every fight night. I probably used the toilet at least five times before every fight — lots of toilet paper too, lol.

It was an honor to fight on such a big platform as K-1 and also to be a main event! There were 7000 people in attendance. As I made my way to the stage, I noticed the production was something next-level: from huge Titantron TVs to DJ Ravidrums. (Look his work up, and you will see all of the superstars he's played for.) Fire, confetti, you name it, this organization had it!

Dewey and I faced off, and I noticed I clearly had the height advantage. Dewey was strong and pressed hard all night. My focus that night, since I had both hands injured, was to throw a lot of kicks, and I did just that. There wasn't a KO this night, but a well-executed fight from both competitors, and I ended up getting my hand raised in victory for the unanimous decision.

Martial artists don't always win, but we keep our head high in defeat just as in victory...Dewey Cooper

---

As I got my hand raised, and the confetti fell from the ceiling, I noticed a little girl in the ring staring at me in anger with her fist balled up, tears running down her face. She had this look as if she was going to truly hurt me. Quickly, Dewey went over and said, "Shaolin! Why are you crying?"

She responded, "I'm mad that he won!"

Dewey replied to his loving and protective daughter: "Yes, he won, and he fought a great fight. I didn't win this time, baby, and that doesn't make me a loser. Randy is a great guy, and I respect him, and you should too! I keep my head high in defeat as I do in victory because that's what martial artists do."

At this point, the tears stopped flowing, and her beautiful smile appeared. Dewey then said, "You should go give Randy a hug, he's a great martial artist just like dad!" Shaolin unrolled her fist and ran over and gave me a hug. That was truly a beautiful moment for me, and a great way to end the show.

Why? Because we live to see another day.

*Martial artists don't always win, but we keep our head high in defeat just as in victory…*Dewey Cooper

Considering that I've been a student, teacher and fighter, the value of respect has been repeatedly honed in me. Respect for myself has been a continual lesson. I decided that it was time to quit eating junk food and staying out all night working as a bouncer at a club. I had some teachers who believed in me and told me I could go further than where I was, and I believed them. As I started winning and growing in my ranks, I kept my disciplined lifestyle. My ritual in training was to get my hands wrapped and get myself mentally ready to have a good practice. To this day, I do self-talk affirmations because I don't want to have crappy practices. You practice the habits you will carry with you into the match…and the match of life.

If I practice good habits of taking care of myself now, and I live in a positive mindset, when I'm 50 years old, I plan to be the in-shape, upbeat man I am now. Obviously, I won't be fighting then, but we all fight something, right? For you, the fight may be your health, or maybe you're fighting for your future, or your family. But whatever your fight is, when you put practices into place to treat yourself well, and they become part of your life, you can fight for the dreams and goals inside of you.

Even though I was a championship winner, I kept myself humble. I went to the gym to work out and didn't strut in like I wanted to be recognized. However, in the rule of respect, every time I walked into the gym, one of the coaches who would be teaching a class would stop his class and say, "Hey guys! It's the heavyweight champion of the world! It's Randy "Boom Boom" Blake!" Every single time.

Martial arts are based on core values
that every student learns.

I would say, "Man, you're embarrassing me. Why are you doing that?" He would remind me that I have 52 wins, 35 knockouts. He would remind me that I was a five-time world champion and a US Martial Arts Hall of Fame inductee. I've been all over the world. I've met Chuck Norris. I live in this city and work out in this gym, so I've earned the respect he's giving. Wow! That was a huge reminder for me. I've not ever forgotten how it makes me feel, and it reminds me why it's also so important for me to show that respect when someone has earned it.

Teaching kids has brought me a lot of joy. I have the opportunity to pass along the same lessons and skills that were taught to me when I was young. I've seen a lot of kids grow up to be extraordinary people. I know it's hard to believe, but students that I taught when they were little come back and tell me, "Hey Mr. Blake, remember me?" I stand there wondering who in the world this 6'4" dude is that is standing in front of me with a full beard and booming deep voice. When they tell me their name, it has always been a shock! They usually say something like, "I thought you were so hard on me all those years ago, giving me push-ups and making me do moves you taught. I've been able to apply the words (that went with the skills) you taught us too. I graduated high school, finished college, and now I own my own business." Or they tell me, "I'm a family man now." To hear a student tell me that if it wasn't for me, they might be on the street selling drugs or something is truly humbling. Martial arts are based on core values that every student learns. "Respect" is one of the tenets that facilitates learning self-respect as well as respecting others. This behavior is expected to be a part of a student's life, on and off the mat. Because of this, respect and martial arts complement each other.

However, you have to learn what respect means in order to put it into practice. Building positivity into your attitude towards others and yourself is key. When you watch a class or competition in martial arts, you will see the students bow to instructors and opponents. There is an air of treating everyone with decency and valuing that person.

Students bow to instructors at the beginning and end of class. This teaches students to recognize the instructor as their leader and to honor their skill. It also shows that there are people in higher positions that have worked hard to get there, and that person deserves consideration for that merit.

Training and competition are intended to be tough, but no matter how vigorous they are, a student is still expected to respect their counterpart. There is a reason rules exist in competition, and the student is taught to obey the rules, bow and shake hands, Students are taught not to perform illegal strikes. That leads to good, healthy competition.

In the same way that respect is part of how a student treats others, a fundamental value is to respect yourself as a person. You'll hear comments from many who've been through martial arts training that it helped to build their self-confidence and worth. When you understand how to serve others with kindness and goodwill, it grows into yourself as well. Respect will be something a martial artist can carry with them for life.

Going back to the idea that respect is an essential part of my training: it truly pays off more than I could have ever imagined. Respect encompasses the will to fight. Sometimes the fight means you are fighting for your life: mentally, physically, emotionally, spiritually. You have to learn how to respect yourself enough to wake up every morning and be ready to fight for what you've been called to do in this life.

You have to learn how to respect yourself enough to wake up every morning and be ready to fight for what you've been called to do in this life.

This isn't about fighting people in a ring or a cage. It's about fighting for what you dream of in your life. Whether or not you feel like it, I encourage you to make the decision to fight depression, anxiety and the voice in your head telling you that you don't deserve to win, that you aren't good enough. The worst thing you can do is to run away from the fight.

When you are faced with a physical fight — maybe you've been diagnosed with a disease or something that seems impossible to overcome — don't quit! It's time to dress up for the fight and show up. Maybe you've had one thing after the other go wrong. Your bank account is empty, your friends have turned against you, you feel like you are done, people have told you it's over. No! No more running and living scared! I want you to fight back, to know that you can take a stand for yourself and put yourself in the situation to say, "Yes! I refuse to be denied!"

The worst thing you can do is to
run away from the fight.

I have faced many battles in my life. I faced the bully that put me in headlocks and spit in my hair when I was a young boy in Ohio. In high school, I faced a guy who made it his aim to leave racist hate notes in my locker every day for weeks to try to intimidate and scare me. I faced all the adolescent moments in Ohio and Oklahoma when I just never felt like I fit in. I got some recognition from the kickboxing arena, but all along I battled physical injuries — a car wreck, torn bicep, surgery and long roads to recovery. I had legal battles, financial battles, fighting depression, isolation and feeling less than. Of course, I'm so grateful for all of the success and lessons, like Nina teaching me to do the hard stuff. I learned that so many people in my life had my back: my family, my friends from high school and my fans. I'm grateful for the opportunity to do what I love, competing in tournaments and matches all over the world. Being inducted into the USA Martial Arts Hall of Fame, all the accolades and opportunities I've been given through the years…I'm so grateful.

All of those moments that I have faced, good and bad, made me the man I am today. Part of my motivation to help others stems from my desire to leave a legacy for my daughter. I want her to understand how vital it is to have respect for herself. I want my daughter to live a model of respect for others. We earn respect from others when we show we respect ourselves.

I love to see someone's face light up when they conquer an obstacle in training during a class. I know how mentally challenging martial arts is and how much it will change a person from not caring about themselves, to understanding the value of their life. That is all about respect. I learned through all the years of my training that respect for my spirit, soul and body was all about treating myself well. Without working out hard and pushing my body to its limit, I could not have had the stamina to fight in the intense world of kickboxing. Without the battles I have dealt with in my life, I could not be here to tell you that YOU can overcome. YOU can make it. YOU can go for your dream. YOU can bring the BOOM!

Randy Blake with Four-Time World Heavyweight Boxing Champion, Evander "The Real Deal" Holyfield.

*Receiving my first "EVERLAST" punching bag
for Christmas in 1993.*

The final kick that earned me the name, "Boom-Boom" in the Chuck Norris World Combat League.

The coaches who made me "World Champion."
Left to right: Peppe Johnson, Michael Jones, Mike Eagan.

Becoming the ISKA World Heavyweight Champion.
June 1, 2012 with Former UFC Light Heavyweight
Champion Jon "Bones" Jones.

Top row:
Mike Eagan, BJ McGee, Jon Jones, Brett Richison,
ISKA President Cory Schafer.

Bottom row:
Lynn Stringfellow, Trey Simpson.

Randy Blake with fight trunks designer,
Miss Ann Clark Slater.

Randy Blake and WWE World Champion,
Bill Goldberg

ROUND FIVE

DISCIPLINE

"Discipline is the foundation upon which all success is built. Lack of discipline inevitably leads to failure." -Jim Rohn

Discipline is one principle that helped me win all five world titles as well as all of my matches. I didn't always have discipline, even though that is something you learn in martial arts and is ingrained in you. Being taught, and living the principle, are two different outcomes. So many times, when we hear the word discipline, we think of it with a negative connotation. Let's change that.

Have you ever heard of animal trainers who use

only positive discipline with their animals? It's true. They reinforce behavior through repetition. The animal is given praise or a reward for the behavior the trainer is requesting. There is not a consequence for something done incorrectly. This is where we've landed so many times with discipline, isn't it? We've equated consequences with discipline, in a negative way. There are positive discipline courses now for parents and kids. Those models are even being implemented in the classroom as well.

There is not a consequence for
something done incorrectly.

Now, let's take a minute to talk about discipline in the realm of goal setting. A lot of people want to change their body in some way: lose weight, gain muscle, be in overall better shape. Or maybe for you, it's trying to incorporate discipline in your finances. Change is hard sometimes, right? This type of discipline is self-discipline. It is the root of being truthful to yourself. It is about keeping your word to yourself. The more you begin to train yourself to incorporate discipline in your life, it actually brings more freedom. Life is constant growth. The constant applying of discipline into your life, day after day, will bring success.

The more you begin to train yourself to incorporate discipline in your life, it actually brings more freedom.

Back when I had my first couple of fights, I won them all by KO in less than one minute. I was still lacking the component of discipline. Why should I train hard if that's how I'm going to perform each and every time, right? I assumed that since I was athletic, that would get me by without having to change the lifestyle that I was choosing to live at that time.

Even though I gave up the job of being a bouncer, I would still go out on weekends with friends. Although I was training in the fighter class, there was only team training twice a week, on Tuesday and Thursday for one hour. It wasn't until I received my first loss during my third pro fight in the Chuck Norris World Combat League that I realized something needed to change. Mike Sheppard was my first loss, and after that loss, he came over and told me, "Great fight, young man, you've got a bright future ahead of you." Later that night at an after-party, I overheard Mike talking with a few of his teammates about what he did to train for his fights. It consisted of training every day. It was like a light bulb switched on at that moment. I immediately went back to the drawing board, and I added training routines every day in my schedule that would lead to winning lots of fights. The more I trained, the more I realized that I had less energy for clubs, parties, etc. Those soon faded, and I quickly gave all of that up. In that moment, I realized that discipline is a combination of sacrifice and integrity.

No one was coming to my house daily to make sure I was going to eat right and exercise above and beyond my regular training routine. No one was coming every day to tell me I could do anything I set my mind to do. It was all going to come from inside of me. In my spirit, soul and body. I was going to have to decide that I was worth it. I didn't have time to wait for someone else to feed my ego. I would have to look in the mirror each day and tell myself that anything was possible. I had to be either all in or all out…and I was ALL IN!

As my caliber of opponent got higher, the more "sacrifice with discipline" became a part of the plan.

Every world-class athlete will tell you that it's about having the edge over your opponent, whether it's in fighting, basketball, football etc. How do you get the edge, if everyone is training full time just like you?

In 2018, I was scheduled to fight for the ISKA World Heavyweight Title against a sharp, hard-hitting, Manny Mancha. He was a southpaw (left-handed) who hit extremely hard and laid his opponents out. He fought, and beat, legit opponents for a major kickboxing league called GLORY.

I was recruited and fought for GLORY as well, and I ended up becoming the first American to win a fight in this league and the first American to win against an international opponent in GLORY by defeating Koichi from Japan.

When it came to sports, early on I focused on basketball skills. I loved to watch games, read about the players and I was a pretty good player myself. My early dream was to be an NBA player. It's natural for me to know a lot of stats about basketball players that I respected most. Take for instance, the 1992 Olympic dream team which featured the likes of Michael Jordan, Magic Johnson and Larry Bird, just to name a few. During the competition, they went on to defeat every team by an average of 44 points on their way to winning the gold medal. Everyone knew the Americans were going to win that year, but part of that reason is they didn't have much real competition. Basketball wasn't as popular internationally.

The story was very different in kickboxing. Americans were not known for competing well against international opponents. Very few Americans, to this day, have international wins on their record.

I knew that in order to beat Manny Mancha, it was going to take discipline to pull off a victory. As I've mentioned before, it takes sacrifice as well as integrity to go with the discipline. I ramped up my training. I was running sprints one day, 3–5 miles the next (most heavyweights don't like to run). I was sparring with nothing but southpaws. My diet consisted of a dozen eggs a day, along with bison, vegetables and water. When it comes to having an edge, you will do what it takes, especially if it means a world title is at stake. I didn't have sex, and yes, you read that right, NO SEX. In the movie, Rocky, coach Mickey tells Rocky, "Women weaken legs!"

Just to give you a list of some World Champions who followed this rule: Muhammad Ali, Joe Frazier, George Forman, Sugar Ray Leonard and Marvin Hagler, to name a few.

That is what I was typically doing for six weeks before fights, but for the Manny fight, I decided to do 12 weeks. I truly wanted to be in the best shape, and I also knew that this guy could potentially give me permanent brain damage. I needed to be on my A-game.

When fight night arrived, we touched gloves out of respect, and we went at it like two beasts! I clearly had the speed advantage, but Manny's power was by far the most intense I had ever tasted in all of my matches. It seemed like the more I hit Manny, the more he kept pressing forward in action. It was like he wanted me to hit him. I hit this man with everything I had. At one point in the fight, I dropped him, but he continued to get up and attack me like a zombie, blood streaming from his face and all. Finally, in the fourth round, I connected a punch on Manny that was a lot like the "hammer" that Mike Sheppard would throw — a looping punch. Itt connected right on Manny's temple and sent him down for the count.

That was one of my greatest victories. Often though, the best part was not always the fight, it was getting your hand raised in victory knowing all of the hard work, discipline and sacrifice paid off. It was amazing to hear:

"YOUR WINNER BY KNOCKOUT,

ANNNND STILLLL

THE ISKA HEAVYWEIGHT

CHAMPION OF THE WORLD!!!

RANDY BOOM-BOOM BLAKE!!!"

FINALLY

Round 1: Courage is key to life itself. It takes courage to act when you've been defeated. It takes courage to start over. If I could do anything for you, I would do my best to inject confidence into you. When you have confidence, the result is courage. There is no limit to your potential. Your potential will go as far as you have the courage to walk. Keep going, the world needs you. Courage is not the absence of fear, it is the triumph over it. F.E.A.R.: Face Everything And Rise. F.E.A.R.: False Evidence Appearing Real. You pick one of those, and make it part of you. If you've lived a life dominated by doubt and fear, it's time to take a step forward and walk into the courage that is yours.

Round 2: Integrity is when you say you're going to do something…you do it. When you honor your word, you earn respect from yourself and from others. Determine that if you talk it, you will walk it. Do the right thing even when no one is watching, and even when we don't feel like it, there is always someone watching. The real prize is the journey on your way to winning whatever battle you face. Doing the right thing leads to better relationships and better outcomes. Have patience on your journey. You are creating a life of legacy when you create a life of integrity. Integrity is telling yourself the truth. Success will come and go, but your word — your integrity — will last forever.

Round 3: Perseverance is faith and believing that you can achieve your goals. The passion to persevere must be a truth that resides in your core. In spite of the setbacks or struggles along your way, be relentless. When you understand that the consistent characteristic of so many who finally achieve their goals isn't that they loved the training or practice. It isn't that they haven't failed. Many times, the difference between the person who achieves their dream and the one who doesn't, is persevering. Setbacks are part of the process, but your passion to succeed must be stronger. As long as you have a dream, you have hope.

Round 4: Respect is a word that I hope you'll plant deep inside of you. When you have a level of respect for the value your life holds, you'll always value the dream inside of you. So many times, we want others to respect us, but really it starts with us respecting ourselves. When you value and respect yourself, you will view others in a different way too. You will value the place they have in your life. Not everyone will be in your life forever, but you can respect the place they hold. Some people come into our lives and lessons and some come as blessings. The blessings are easy because we all like to be blessed. The lessons are a little harder because no one likes to be uncomfortable. Showing love to yourself by treating yourself well, whether that means eating healthy food, getting enough sleep, moving your body with some form of exercise or talking to a therapist if you need it…that's a beautiful form of respect. I hope you'll incorporate it regularly into your life.

Round 5: Discipline is about positivity. Sometimes, it has been given a bad rap because we equate it with denying ourselves something we might enjoy. But not so. Discipline is about ownership. It is taking responsibility for your life and the path that you're on. Are you doing things right now that are propelling your life forward or backward? Are you making progress or are you stagnant? The difference between you and me, and the place we want to be…is a small distance that is about discipline. Training our mind is as important as training our body. If we are willing to use our mind to understand that when we tell ourselves we are going to do something, we will do it. We will summon courage, integrity, perseverance and respect, and carry it through with discipline to achieve our goals and dreams!

LETTER TO ROGUE MARCELLA BLAKE

Baby girl,

To go your own way, full of strength and courage, ready to go to war…this is what your name means.

I hope that you wear it every day with greatness. You came into this world 2/3/2021, 11:39 pm, at 10lb, 11oz.

You came into this world strong like a champion. Baby girl, you are my most precious gift.

My life was permanently transformed on the day you arrived on this planet. I've been blessed beyond measure, and having you here is just another reminder of that.

So many individuals extol their "things" and let

their feelings about themselves be dictated by the car they drive, the clothes they wear or how others see them, among other things. Many celebrities sell their souls for money, fame or acceptance from a particular "culture." This is why you will be prepared. You are a warrior princess. If your self-worth is based on other people or things that money can purchase, you will never be great. No one can take away your greatness because it already exists within you.

Daddy loves you — always.
Randy Marick Blake Jr.

ACKNOWLEDGMENTS

Randy Blake Sr. and Kim Blake:

Big thank you to both of my parents for your guidance, love and parenting in helping me become the man that I am today. You guys are my biggest fans, and I am so grateful that you have literally seen all of my fights, whether it was at home or traveling to another state/country. Mom, thank you for planting the seed to grow. Dad, you had the most important job and everyone should know this. Sacrifice is one of the hardest things in life, especially when all the chips are in one's hand. You sacrificed everything so that my brother Gerald and I could have the chance at becoming great in this world. That principle alone is what it truly means to be a father, living for something or someone greater than yourself. I will make sure to pass this baton on to my beautiful daughter. I love the both of you.

Miss Ann.

You were the brains and operation behind the Boom fight trunks. It was truly a blessing to cross paths with you, and I appreciate all 37 pairs of trunks, dating back to 2009, that you have made custom. I think about you often, and if you were still alive, you'd be proud of the work that Denna has done on my most recent trunks. I want to thank both of you for making my fights that much easier. You cared about my vision and the story told when I would wear each pair of those trunks. Thank you.

I want to thank my sponsors:

Dave Owens with HST (Hand Speed Trainer); Chuck Zoellner (Zoellner Chiropractic); Chera Kimiko (Kimiko medical aesthetics).

Thank you for all of your support throughout this long journey of a career. Many sponsors have come and gone, but you were the few that have ridden the whole journey, and I can't thank you enough for the providing of your services to aid in giving me the edge in my performances. For that, I truly consider you all family.

Joe "Gunny Ski" Pawlowski:

We met in martial arts class when I was fifteen, and that's truly when I knew that I had a lifelong friend. Thank you for being the best bodyguard any man could ever ask for. Also, thank you for enduring some of the intense training that I had to go through in order to prepare for world title bouts. I always appreciated you even being in my corner as a coach. It meant a lot. You took care of me and always had my back, just like a real brother would. Above all, I want to say thank you for your service to this country. That is what makes you the real hero.

Sylvester Meola:

After being bullied and taking up martial arts, it's an honor to say that you gave me my first lesson. You were the first instructor to equip that 6-year-old boy with confidence and many other life skills that martial arts teaches. If you were alive today, I'd hope that you would be proud of the man that I've become today and all that I have accomplished. Thank you for the lighting of the torch that still burns and shines bright today.

Mike Jones:

Not the rapper, Mike Jones, but Mike Jones, the former fighter himself. We met when I was invited to "fight class." We've trained together and even bounced at clubs together, and I wanted to say thank you for being an influence in the decision making that would ultimately lead me to world titles. You are a friend, a brother and even a coach who has cornered me. Thank you for all of the memories created, and I look forward to many more.

Codale Ford:

Late in my career, I seldom had the chance to travel the world to get world-class sparring. I can say that you were the most consistent sparring partner I had to prepare for the most important fights in my career. While those big guys ran, you chose to embrace many sparring wars with me, even though you're only 5'9", 170lb. I wanted to make sure to let you know that I'll always have the utmost respect for you. Thank you.

Dale Cook:

I got my start on one of your local shows at the Greenwood Cultural Center. Thank you for giving me a chance to showcase on a local show. That led me to experience bigger fights in the major leagues of kickboxing, among the elites.

Coach Mike Eagan:

You were my very first coach in kickboxing, and it was truly an honor to have learned most of the skill sets from you. I used them in many fights. We won our first world title in 2012, along with help from Brett, BJ and Lynn. Thank you, guys, for all of the hours spent in preparation.

Alger Flood:

You were my principal in the 9th grade. You were definitely the best principal; what made you great is that you took the time to always ask me how I was doing. You always gave words of encouragement, and those are principles that I carry with me as I now mentor the younger generation. Thank you for being kind and thank you for speaking words of wisdom to that young kid who was a lone soul at the time.

David "Master Kick" Vogtman

I truly believe YOU had the most influence on all that I've accomplished today. Thank you for demonstrating persistence in getting me to class. These are values that I teach to this day. You taught me how words can lift us up or tear us down. In your case, you've impacted me to become something extraordinary that I couldn't even see in myself, and I'll always make sure that you get credit for that.

Coach Peppe Johnson:

In 2014, after a hard fought loss, I was ready to retire and move on in life. After connecting with you, there was a resurgence in my career, and with you in my corner, we went on to win the ISKA title four more times. You are the reason I am a five-time World Champion. You simply believed in me. You taught me to always hold myself accountable. You taught me to always push hard in training. What sticks out the most, is that you're not just a coach inside the cage/ring, but an amazing coach at life. I've seen up close how greatly invested you are in being a father. These principles are what make real champions. Thank you for being a great mentor in my life.

To all of my fans:

I can't express how thankful I am to have had each and every one of you in my life. Without you, my career wouldn't exist. I am thankful for literally every ticket sold, even if it was the worst seat. For flying all over the United States, and all the way to Japan, I want to say thank you all for being on this journey with me.

Special Thanks to OSTEOSTRONG˙
Tulsa Midtown for Their Support of this Book

What is

OSTEO⊗STRONG®

A Unique System For Developing Your Skeletal Strength:

OsteoStrong® is not a gym, diet, supplement, pharmaceutical, or a medical treatment. OsteoStrong® is a unique place where you can go to improve your overall health by focusing on the one thing we all have in common: a skeletal system.

The skeletal system is the foundation for your body and provides more than just strength and protection. It is arguably one of the most critical systems of the human body, and by implementing a strategy to care for and strengthen it, many experience the following results:

- Improved Bone Density
- Improved Posture
- Improved Balance
- Improved Athletic Performance
- Less Joint and Back Pain

OsteoStrong® works for people at all ages and levels of activity to promote skeletal strength which impacts the entire body in many ways using a process known as Osteogenic Loading. Sessions are quick, painless, and results are measurable and happen quickly. There are a few things to know prior to coming in your first time so that you can make the best of the experience.

Osteostrong˙ is Featured in Tony Robbins New Book:

"One of the greatest tools I have
ever seen in my life."
Tony Robbins

Find Out What OsteoStrong˙ Can Do For You!
Visit www.OsteoStrong.me

OsteoStrong˙
Tulsa Midtown
918-528-3828
5940 S. Lewis Ave
Tulsa, OK 74105

Made in the USA
Columbia, SC
08 June 2022

61490690R00061